1·2·3 Draw
CARTOON ALIENS
AND SPACE STUFF

A step-by-step Guide

By Steve Barr

Peel Productions, Inc

This book is dedicated to my friend Nora Smith,
who always makes me laugh and loves books!

Library of Congress Cataloging-in-Publication Data
Barr, Steve.
  1-2-3 draw cartoon aliens and space stuff : a step-by-step guide / by Steve Barr.
    v. cm.
Contents: Before you begin -- Basic shapes and lines -- Alien head (side view) -- Alien head (front view) -- Alien expressions (side view) -- Alien expressions (front view) -- Alien bodies (side view) -- Alien bodies (front view) -- Sitting aliens -- Floating alien -- Alien disguised as a human -- Flying saucer -- Spaceship -- Space scooter -- Planet, comets and stars -- Astronaut -- Robot -- Space worm -- Fun stuff.
  ISBN 0-939217-71-6 (alk. paper : pbk.)
  1. Life on other planets in art--Juvenile literature. 2. Space vehicles in art--Juvenile literature. 3. Drawing--Technique--Juvenile literature. [1. Extraterrestrial beings in art. 2. Space vehicles in art. 3. Drawing--Technique.] I. Title: One-two-three draw cartoon aliens and space stuff. II. Title: Cartoon aliens and space stuff. III. Title.
  NC825.O9 B37 2003
  741.5--dc21   2002013990

Distributed to the trade and art markets in North America by

NORTH LIGHT BOOKS,
an imprint of F&W Publications, Inc.
4700 East Galbraith Road
Cincinnati, OH 45236

(800) 289-0963

Contents

Before you begin...

You will need the following supplies:

1. A pencil (or pencils!)
2. An eraser
3. A pencil sharpener
4. LOTS of paper
5. Colored pencils, markers or crayons
6. A good light source
7. A comfortable place to draw
8. Your imagination!

Are you ready?

Let's draw!

No rules!

One of the most fun things about drawing cartoons is that there are NO RULES! Cartoons are just simple drawings using basic shapes and lines to create a funny picture. Cartoons are meant to make people laugh or smile. The sillier your cartoon looks the better.

When I was young, I spent hours sketching and doodling, and drawing cartoons. I got so good that I get paid to draw cartoons now. In this book you will learn how to draw really cool aliens and space stuff. You will be surprised at how easy it is to do once you start drawing.

Sketch, doodle, play!

Have fun. Experiment! If I tell you to draw a circle and you feel like drawing a square or a triangle, draw whatever you want. Make your very own creation. Change anything you want. Color your cartoon any color you wish. Create your own cartoon style. Draw to entertain your friends and family, and one day you may end up getting paid to do it too!

Cartooning Tips:

1 Draw lightly at first — SKETCH, so you can erase extra lines.

2 Practice, practice, practice! You will get better and your cartoons will get funnier.

3 Have fun cartooning!

Basic Shapes and Lines

Here are some of the simple shapes and lines you will use to draw cartoon aliens:

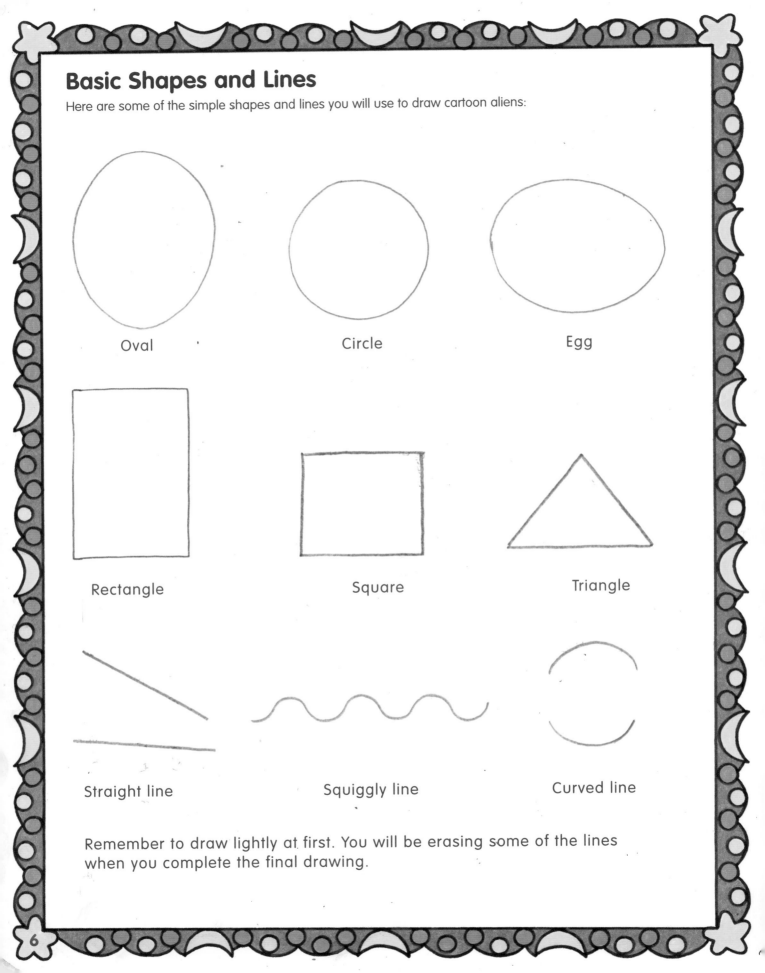

Oval

Circle

Egg

Rectangle

Square

Triangle

Straight line

Squiggly line

Curved line

Remember to draw lightly at first. You will be erasing some of the lines when you complete the final drawing.

Alien head (side view)

Let's start by drawing just the head of an alien. A little later in this book, I will show you how to add the body. Since none of us really knows what an alien looks like, let's use our imagination and draw aliens that we would like to meet.

1 Sketch a big oval for the head. Sketch two smaller ovals for the nose and eye.

2 Draw a small oval inside the eye. Sketch an overlapping oval for the ear.

3 Darken part of the eye. Draw a small curved line for a smiling mouth. Sketch another oval on the ear.

4 Add a curved line to the mouth. Draw a slightly curved line inside the ear.

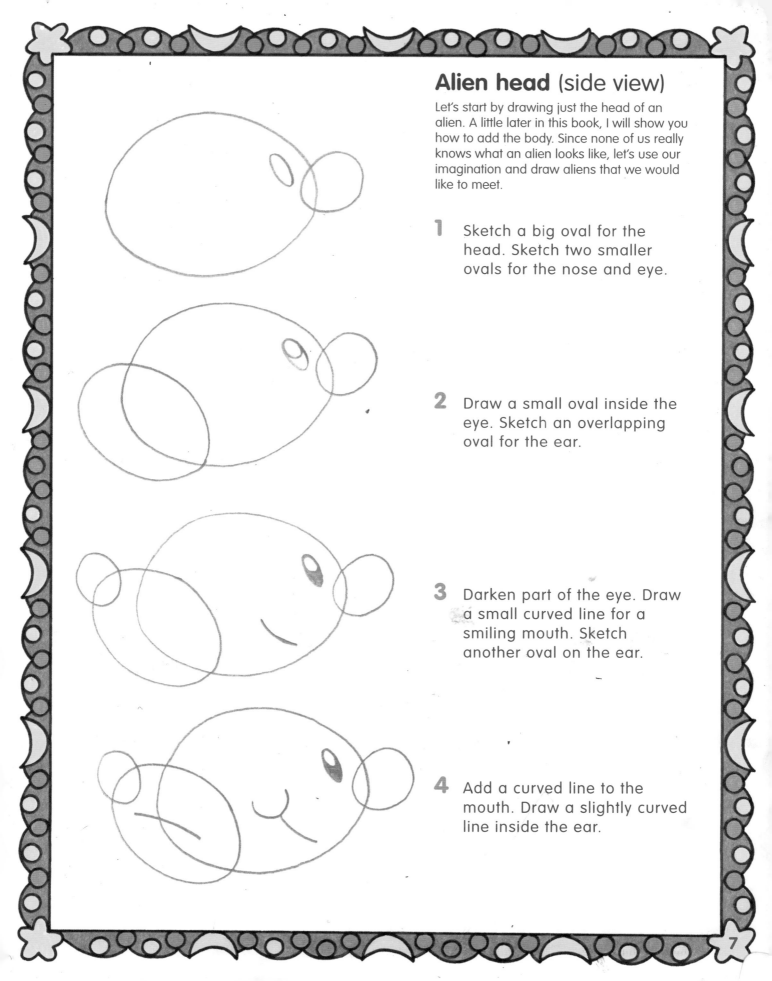

5 Draw four straight lines to begin his antenna. Add another curved line to the alien's mouth.

6 Add a circle to the end of the antenna. Draw another curved line inside his mouth.

7 LOOK at the final drawing! Erase extra sketch lines you don't need. Darken the final lines. Add color. Add triangles or squares or any fun features you wish.

Adorable alien!

GREAT JOB!
Sign your name and put today's date on your work. It lets everyone know you drew it!

Alien head (front view)

Let's draw an alien looking right at you.

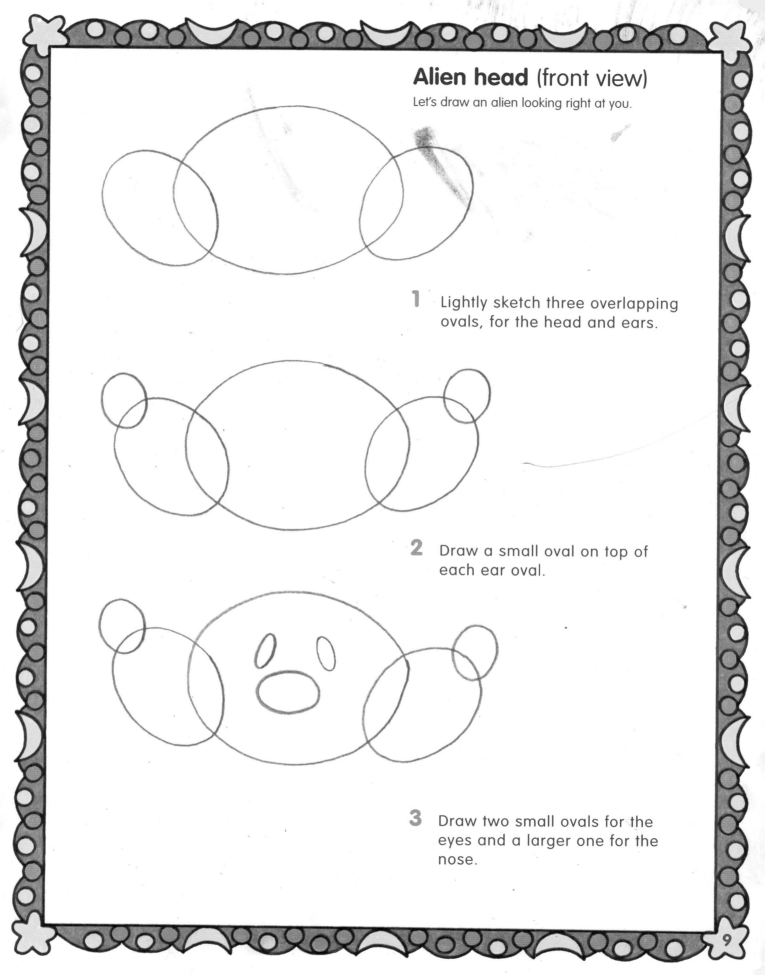

1 Lightly sketch three overlapping ovals, for the head and ears.

2 Draw a small oval on top of each ear oval.

3 Draw two small ovals for the eyes and a larger one for the nose.

4 Add a small oval inside each eye. Draw a curved line for his mouth.

5 Darken in part of the eyes. Add a curved line to each side of his mouth.

6 Draw two straight lines on the top of his head, to begin the antenna. Draw a curved line inside each of the ears.

7 Add two slightly curved lines and a circle to the complete the antenna.

8 LOOK at the final drawing! Erase extra sketch lines. Darken the final lines. Add color.

WOW!!!
Experiment with colors and shapes to see how different you can make him look.

Alien expressions (side view)

You can bring your alien to life by drawing different expressions to show how he is feeling. Here are some examples of facial expressions you can easily draw with simple shapes and lines.

LOOK closely at the different expressions shown below. Can you see the simple shapes and lines that are used to show what mood he is in?

Start with a sketch of the outline of the alien's head.

Sketch your favorite expressions a few times and then try to create a new expression of your own.

Alien expressions (front view)

LOOK carefully at the different expressions shown below. See the shapes and lines that are used to create the different moods.

Draw the outline of the alien's head from the front.

Now draw three or four of the expressions you see.

Experiment! Using different shapes, see what expressions you can create!

Alien (side view)

Let's draw a complete alien—head to toe.

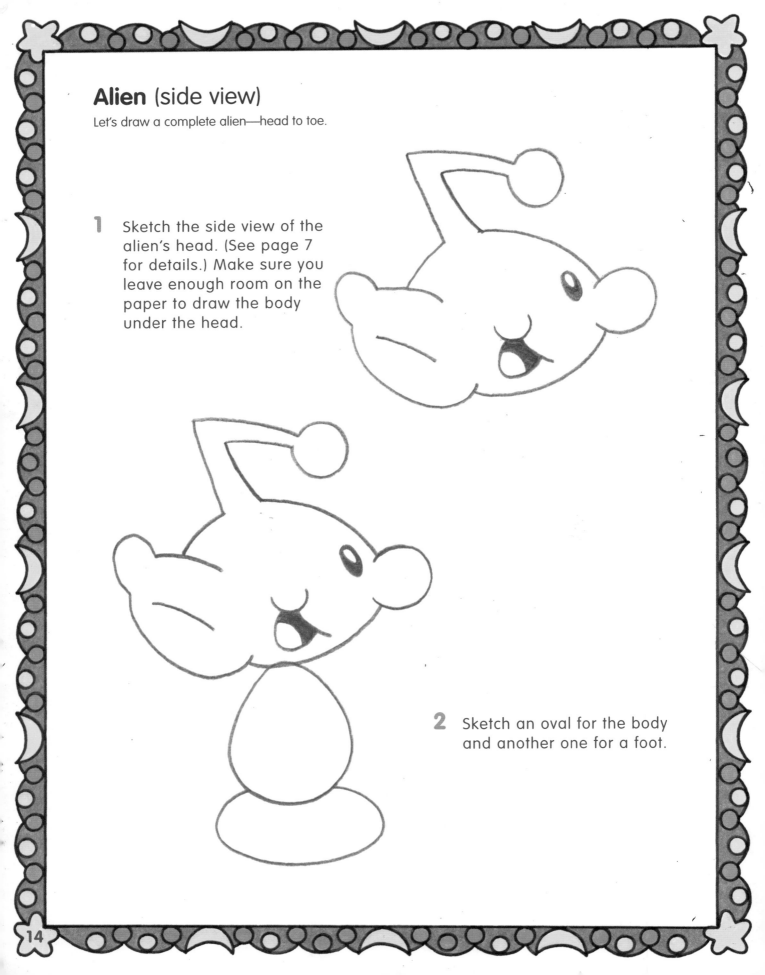

1 Sketch the side view of the alien's head. (See page 7 for details.) Make sure you leave enough room on the paper to draw the body under the head.

2 Sketch an oval for the body and another one for a foot.

3 Sketch an oval for the arm. Draw a curved line for the other foot.

4 Sketch three small ovals for fingers. Draw squiggly lines on the bottom of his feet.

5 Draw curved lines across his feet.

6 Draw two straight lines with a circle on the end for his left arm and hand.

7 Sketch four ovals for fingers on the left hand.

8 LOOK at the final drawing! Erase extra sketch lines. Darken the final lines. Add color.

Nice job!
You are getting to be quite a talented cartoonist. Keep practicing and you will get even better.

Alien (front view)

I think you are ready for a challenge. Let's draw an alien facing you.

1 Draw the front view of the alien's head again. (See page 9 for details.) Make sure you leave plenty of room under his head to add a body.

2 Draw a curved line for his body. Sketch two overlapping ovals for his shoes.

3 Draw two straight lines for arms, on each side of the body. Add a curved line under both of the shoe ovals.

4 Sketch circles for hands at the end of each arm. Draw a small rectangle in the center of his body, to begin a belt buckle. Sketch two curved lines on the ends of each of each shoe.

5 Sketch four ovals on each hand for fingers. Draw another smaller rectangle inside the buckle. Draw two lines on each side for the belt.

6 LOOK at the final drawing! Erase extra sketch lines. Darken the final lines. Add color.

Friendly alien! Does he want a hug?

Sitting alien (side view)

Even aliens get tired every now and then and have to take a break. Let's draw an alien sitting down and relaxing.

1 Sketch three ovals — for the head, nose, and body.

2 Sketch two overlapping ovals for his ear. Sketch another oval to begin a big shoe.

3 Draw a small oval for his eye. Darken part of it. Draw two straight lines on the body oval for an arm.

4 Draw two curved lines on top of his head, to begin his antenna. Draw two small curved lines for his smiling mouth. Sketch an oval for his hand.

5 Add two more lines and a circle to complete his antenna. Draw a straight line and a curved line in his ear. Draw a curved line for his other shoe. Sketch an oval for his thumb. Add two straight lines for fingers.

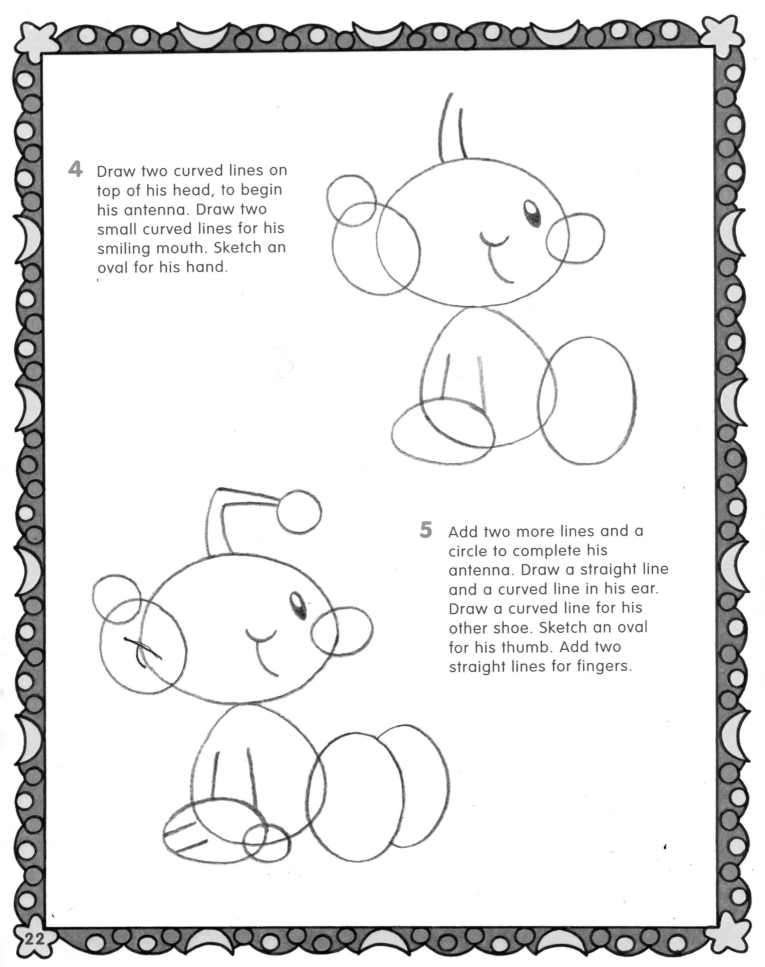

6 Draw two curved lines, for soles on his shoes. Draw straight lines on the soles.

7 LOOK at this drawing! Erase any extra sketch lines. Darken the final lines. Add a series of connected curved lines, below your alien, to make a cloud for him to rest on.

8 Add color.

Wow! You are becoming a talented cartoonist really quickly!

Floating alien

I have read that aliens can levitate. That means they can float in the air. I wish I could do that. It seems like it would be a lot of fun. Let's make our alien levitate.

1 LOOK closely at this drawing. The bottom oval is not straight under the head this time. It leans to one side. Sketch the three ovals — for the head, nose and body.

2 Draw an oval for the eye. Darken part of it. Sketch an oval to begin his ear. Sketch an oval for one shoe.

3 Draw two curved lines for his mouth. Sketch a small circle on the top of his ear. Draw a curved line for the other shoe.

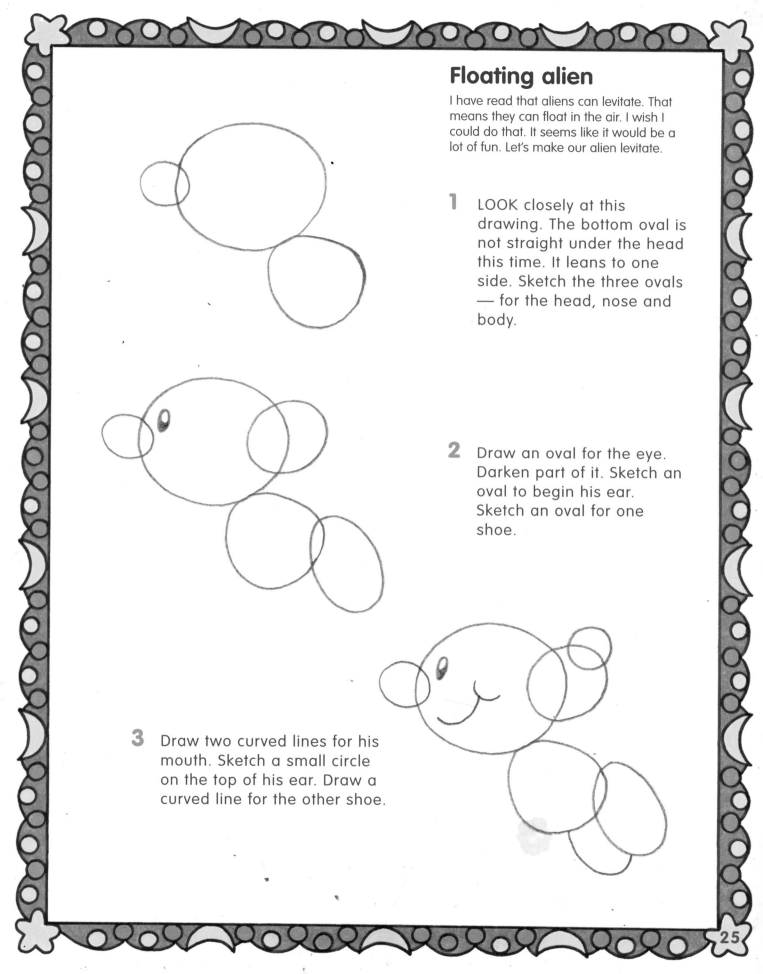

4 Draw two curved lines on top of his head to begin his antenna. Add another curved line to his mouth. Draw a curved line inside his ear. Add a curved line to the bottom of each shoe.

5 Draw the lines and a circle to complete the antenna. Darken part of the mouth. Draw three straight lines to begin his arms. Add two curved lines to the top of each shoe.

6 LOOK at his hands! Add curved and straight lines to make his hands and fingers.

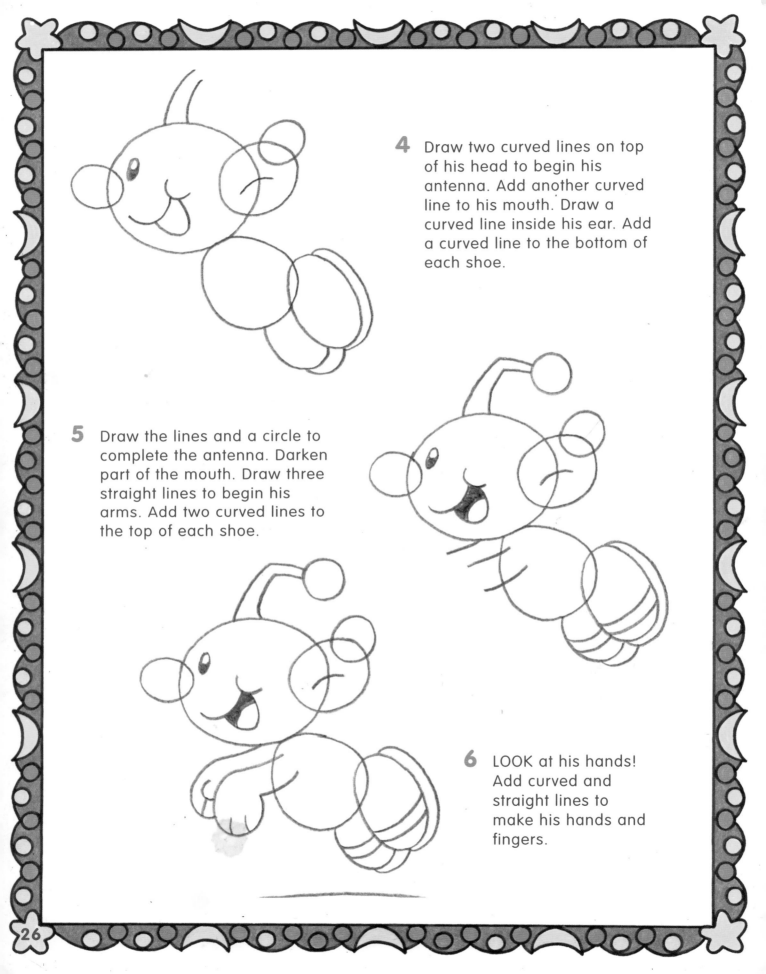

7 Draw a curved line and a long thin oval beneath him.

8 LOOK carefully at the final drawing! Erase extra sketch lines. Darken the final lines. Draw a few curved lines around him to make him look like he is floating above the surface of a planet! Add color. Is he floating above a lake, or is it his shadow?

Alien disguised as a human

When aliens visit our planet, they are sometimes afraid that humans might capture them. I have heard rumors that they sometimes wear clothing like earthlings to try to blend in while they are here. Let's draw an alien in a human disguise!

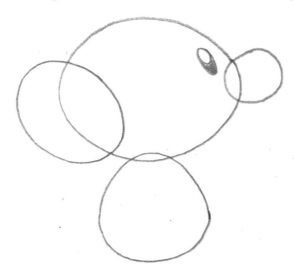

1 Sketch three overlapping ovals for his head, ear, and nose. Sketch a small oval for his eye. Darken part of the eye. Sketch an oval for the body.

2 Sketch a small circle on top of his ear. Draw two curved lines for a mouth. Sketch an oval for a shoe.

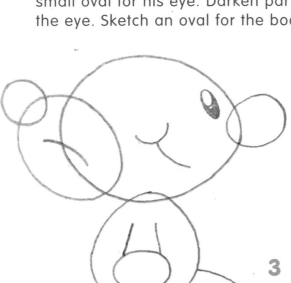

3 Draw a curved line inside his ear. Draw two straight lines and an oval for his arm and hand. Draw a curved line for his other foot.

4 Sketch three ovals on the hand for fingers. Draw a curved line on the bottom of each shoe for soles.

5 Draw four curved lines to begin his hat. Draw a curved line for his shirt sleeve and a curved line on each side of his arm, for his shirt bottom. Draw two curved lines on the top of each shoe.

6 Draw four more curved lines, an oval, and two circles to complete the hat.

7 LOOK at the final drawing! Erase extra sketch lines. Darken the final lines. Add color.

Clever alien!

Alien flying a saucer

Aliens like to use a lot of fancy machines to fly around exploring earth and outer space. One of their favorites is a flying saucer. So sharpen your pencils and let's draw one!

1 Sketch an oval for the alien's head and an oval for his nose. Draw two straight lines for his neck. Draw an oval around his neck to begin the flying saucer. Draw a larger oval for the outside of the saucer.

2 Sketch an oval for his ear. Draw a curved line on each side of his neck for the inside of the saucer. Draw a long curved line on the side of the saucer.

3 Sketch two slightly curved lines, on top of his head, to begin his antenna. Draw an oval for an eye. Darken part of the eye. Sketch a small circle on top of his ear.

Darken part of the saucer opening, on each side of his neck. Sketch small circles along the big curved line. Leave some space between each of them.

4 Add two curved lines to his antenna. Draw a curved line inside his ear. Draw two straight lines for his arm.

5 Draw a circle to complete his antenna. Draw two small curved lines to make his mouth.

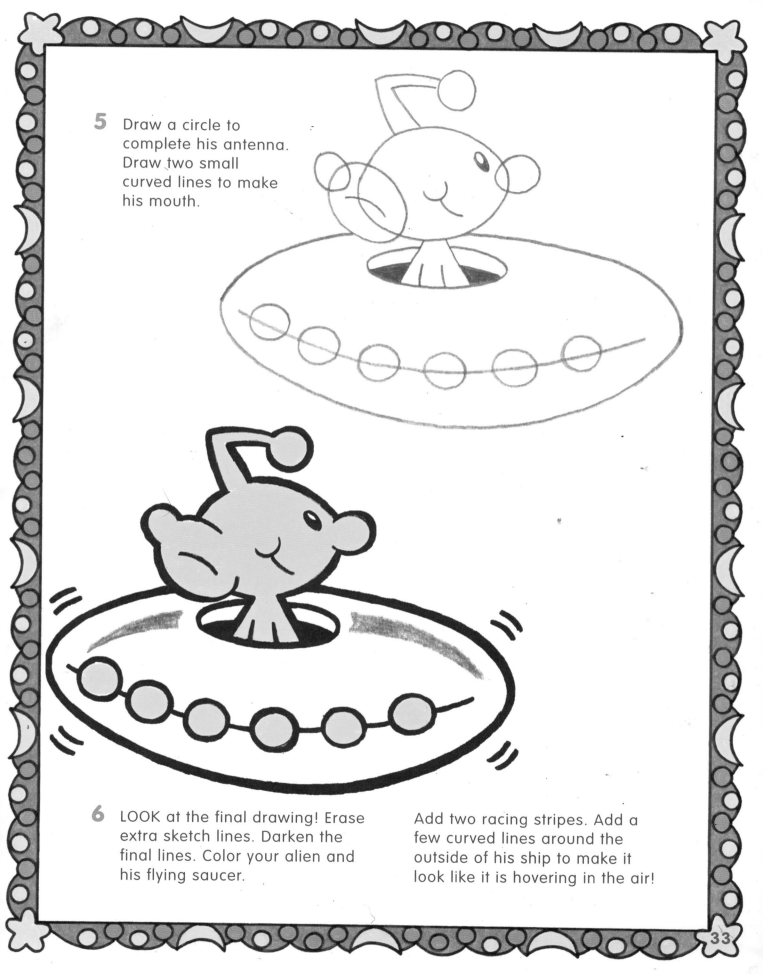

6 LOOK at the final drawing! Erase extra sketch lines. Darken the final lines. Color your alien and his flying saucer.

Add two racing stripes. Add a few curved lines around the outside of his ship to make it look like it is hovering in the air!

Alien in a spaceship

Some aliens have fancier ships than others. Aliens actually consider flying saucers to be old-fashioned now, so let's try drawing a fancier, more modern spaceship. Start your drawing in the middle of the page, so you have plenty of room.

1 Sketch an oval for the alien's head. Draw two straight lines for his neck. Draw another straight line to begin the opening of the spaceship.

2 Draw a curved line, on each side of the head, for the side of the spaceship. Add two slightly curved, connecting lines for the spaceship's opening.

3 Sketch an oval for his nose. LOOK at the shape of the ship! Draw two connecting curved lines to complete the main section of the ship. Draw two straight lines inside the spaceship opening.

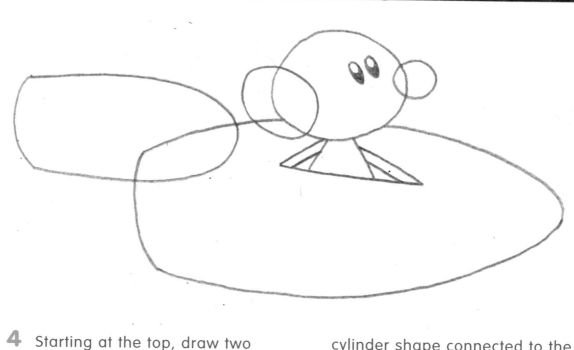

4 Starting at the top, draw two small ovals for his eyes. Darken part of each eye. Sketch an oval to begin his ear. LOOK at the cylinder shape connected to the body of the spaceship. Using curved lines, sketch the cylinder.

5 Draw two curved lines to begin his antenna. Add a small circle to the top of his ear. Draw a curved line on the side of his ship. Add two curved lines to the front of his spacecraft.

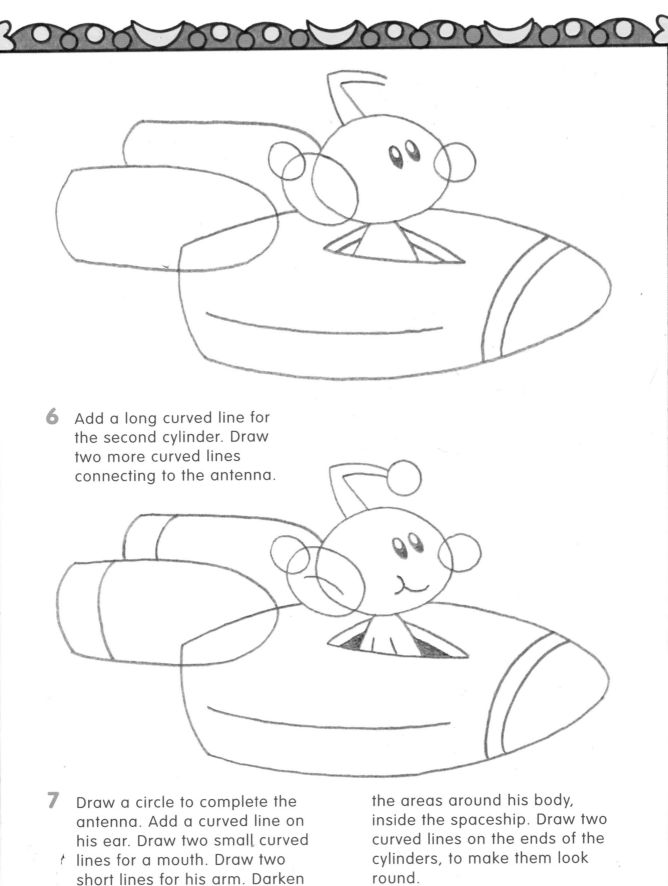

6 Add a long curved line for the second cylinder. Draw two more curved lines connecting to the antenna.

7 Draw a circle to complete the antenna. Add a curved line on his ear. Draw two small curved lines for a mouth. Draw two short lines for his arm. Darken the areas around his body, inside the spaceship. Draw two curved lines on the ends of the cylinders, to make them look round.

8 LOOK at the final drawing! Erase extra sketch lines. Darken the final lines. Add some straight lines behind his head and the spaceship to make it look like it is flying fast. Add color.

CONGRATULATIONS!

Great job! You just drew an amazing alien and spaceship.
Sign your name to your drawing and put today's date on it.
Hang it on your wall.

Alien space scooter

Young aliens like to explore new planets when their family visits them, but they are not old enough to drive a spaceship. So they usually rent a space scooter that they use to get around. Let's draw one.

1 Sketch three overlapping ovals for the alien's head, nose and ear. Sketch an oval for his body. Sketch another oval for a shoe.

2 Draw an oval for the eye. Darken part of it. Sketch a small circle on the top of his ear. Draw a curved line on the bottom of his foot.

3 Draw two straight lines on top of his head, to begin his antenna. Draw two straight lines for his arm. Draw two curved lines for his other shoe.

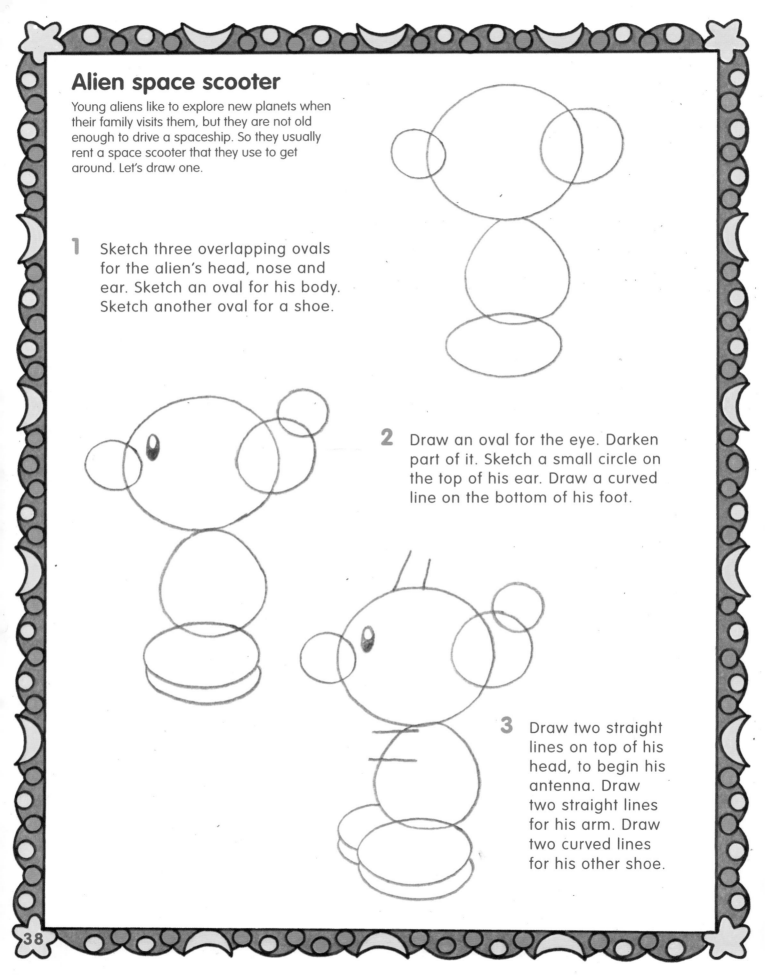

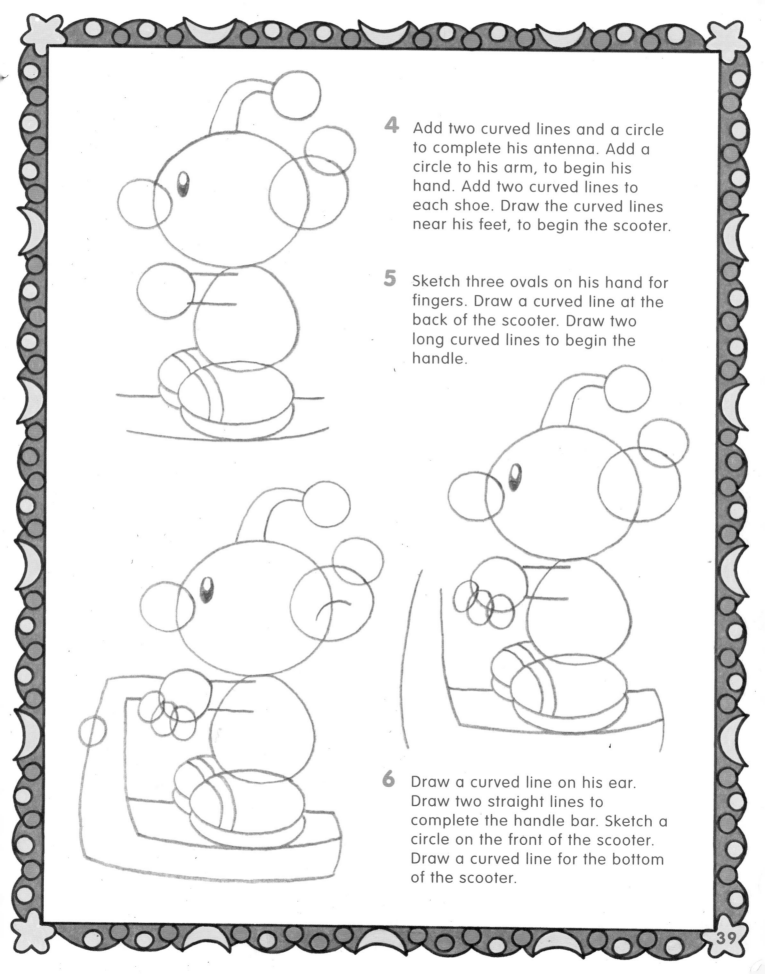

4 Add two curved lines and a circle to complete his antenna. Add a circle to his arm, to begin his hand. Add two curved lines to each shoe. Draw the curved lines near his feet, to begin the scooter.

5 Sketch three ovals on his hand for fingers. Draw a curved line at the back of the scooter. Draw two long curved lines to begin the handle.

6 Draw a curved line on his ear. Draw two straight lines to complete the handle bar. Sketch a circle on the front of the scooter. Draw a curved line for the bottom of the scooter.

7 LOOK closely at his mouth. Draw four curved lines to form his mouth. Draw two straight lines and one curved line for the scooter's tailpipe. Using curved lines, draw flames.

8 LOOK at the final drawing! Erase extra sketch lines. Darken the final lines. Color your alien and his space scooter. Add a few straight lines behind him to make it look like he is moving fast.

Planets, comets, and stars

Let's draw some of the objects our alien will encounter in space. After you learn how to draw them, you can sketch a picture with these space objects in the background.

1 Sketch a large circle. If you have trouble drawing a good circle, it is okay to trace something round. Try a jar lid or a plastic cup.

2 Sketch four ovals inside the circle.

3 Draw a curved line inside each oval. Draw three curved lines on the left side of your circle.

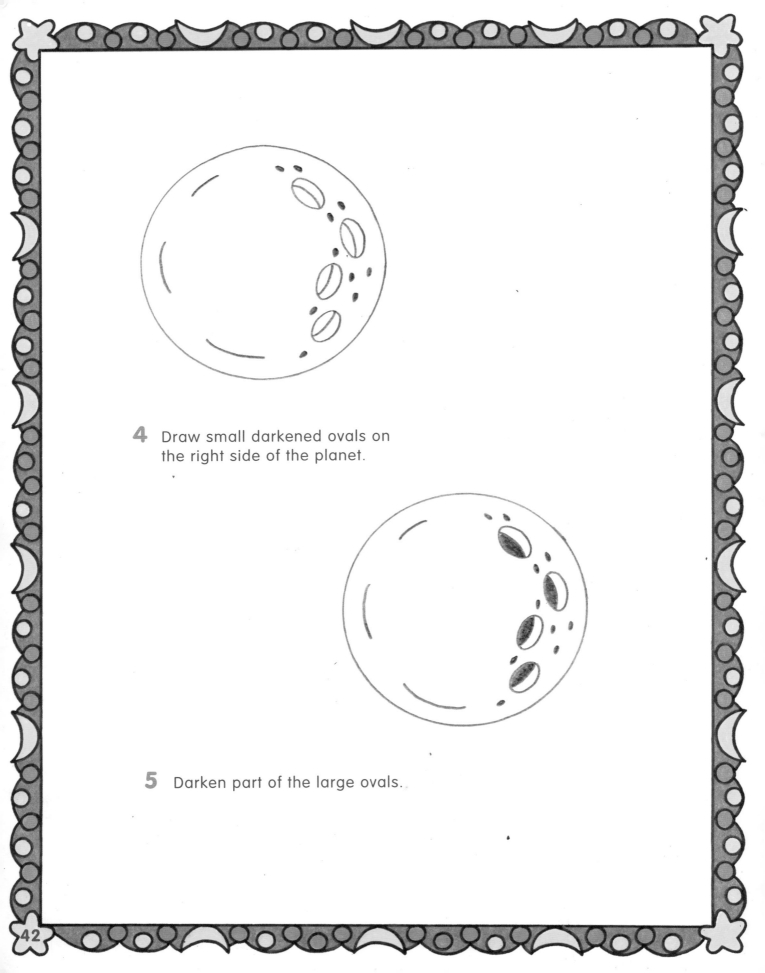

4 Draw small darkened ovals on the right side of the planet.

5 Darken part of the large ovals.

6 Draw small connecting curved lines around the outside of the planet. This will give it a rugged look.

7 LOOK at the final drawing! Erase extra sketch lines. Darken the final lines. Color your planet any color you want. Check out the word "planet" in the encyclopedia to see how different planets look. Or just make up your own colors.

Pretty planet!
There are many different types of planets in the universe. Since this is a new one, and you created it, try to think of a name for it.

Let's draw a comet. It will start out as a
planet. Start your drawing in the center
of your paper so you will have room to
draw the comet's tail.

1 Draw the planet shape
again.

2 Draw long squiggly lines
trailing off the back side,
getting closer to each other
the further away they get
from the planet, which is a
comet.

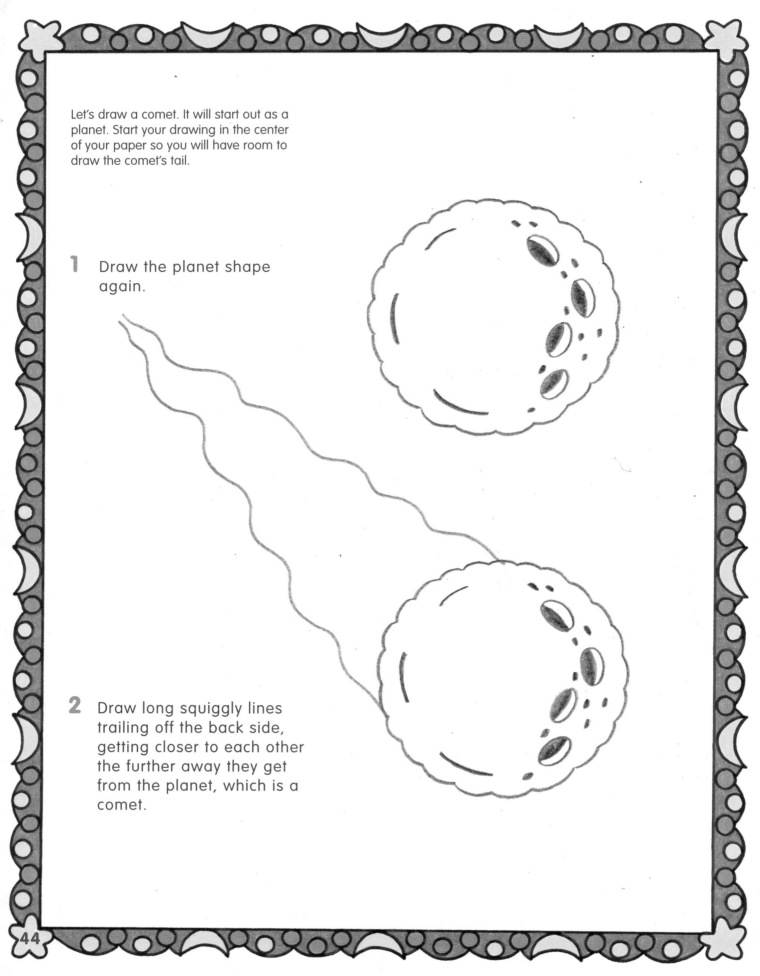

3 Draw curved lines and squiggly lines to create flames alongside the comet's tail.

4 Draw curved lines around the outside of the comet to make it look like it is shaking. Draw three squiggly lines over the comet and tail.

5 LOOK at the final drawing! Color your comet and its tail. Imagine this flying through space.

Super comet!

There are many different kinds of planets in the universe. Not all planets look alike.

Let's draw another planet. We will start with a circle again. Remember that it is okay for you to use a round object to draw a good circle.

1 Sketch a large circle.

2 Draw two long curved lines circling your planet.

3 LOOK at the final drawing! Erase extra sketch lines. Add color.

Let's draw a simple star.

1 Sketch an upside-down valentine.

2 Draw curved lines on each side.

3 LOOK at the final drawing! Erase extra sketch lines. Color your star any color you wish.

When you draw cartoons, you can turn any object into a living thing. Here are some fun faces you can draw on your star, using simple shapes and lines, to bring it to life! Try drawing these.

Astronaut

Let's draw a space explorer.

1 Sketch an oval for the head. Draw a curved line under it for the neck. Draw a large partial oval for the body. Draw three straight lines for the legs.

2 Draw a curved line in the middle of the top oval. Sketch a long oval for the arm. Draw an oval for one shoe. Draw a curved line behind it for the other shoe.

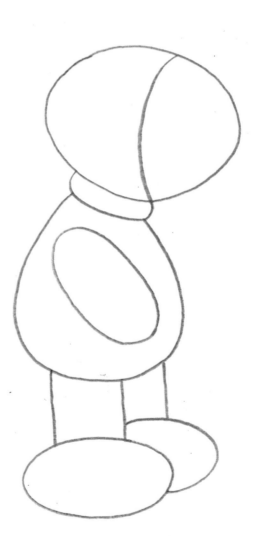

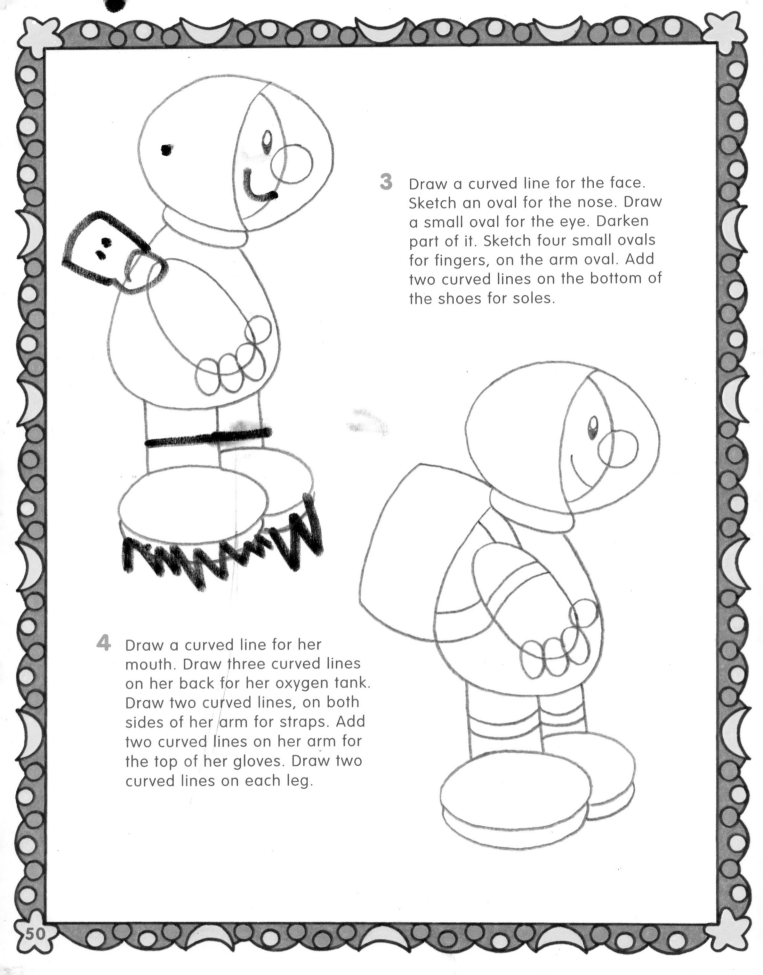

3 Draw a curved line for the face. Sketch an oval for the nose. Draw a small oval for the eye. Darken part of it. Sketch four small ovals for fingers, on the arm oval. Add two curved lines on the bottom of the shoes for soles.

4 Draw a curved line for her mouth. Draw three curved lines on her back for her oxygen tank. Draw two curved lines, on both sides of her arm for straps. Add two curved lines on her arm for the top of her gloves. Draw two curved lines on each leg.

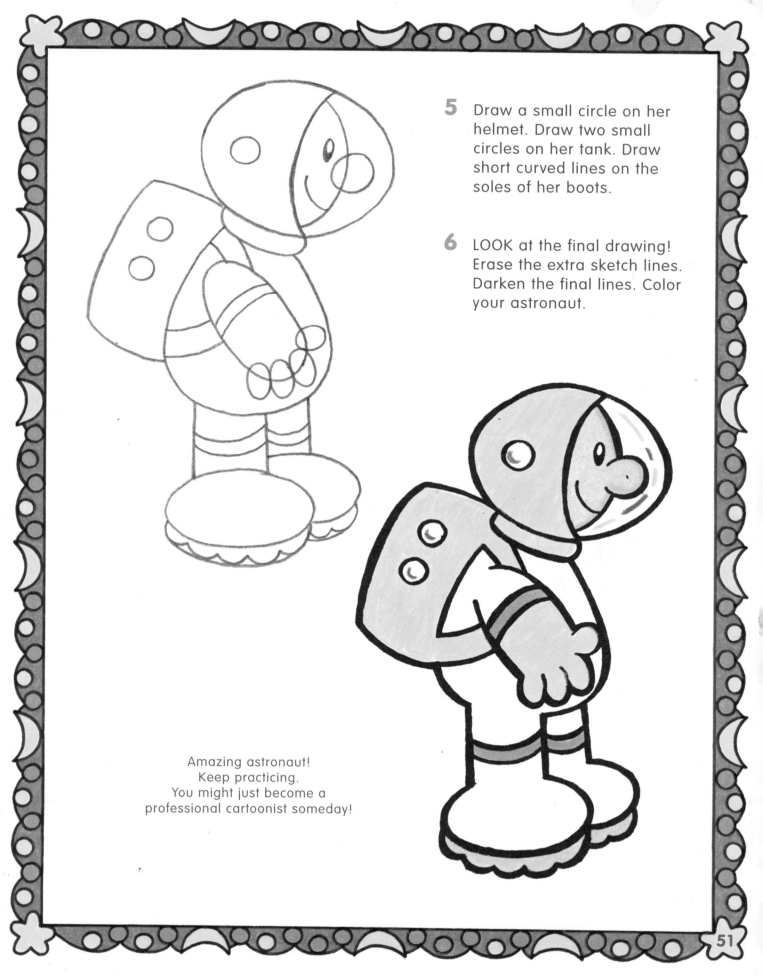

5 Draw a small circle on her helmet. Draw two small circles on her tank. Draw short curved lines on the soles of her boots.

6 LOOK at the final drawing! Erase the extra sketch lines. Darken the final lines. Color your astronaut.

Amazing astronaut!
Keep practicing.
You might just become a
professional cartoonist someday!

Space monster

Sometimes an alien will run into a space monster on his travels. Let's draw a really nasty one.

1 LOOK at the kidney-shaped body. Sketch it. Draw four short, straight lines for legs. Sketch an oval at the bottom of each leg for feet.

2 Sketch two large ovals for eyes. Sketch four ovals on each foot for toes.

3 Draw a small oval inside each eye. Darken part of it. Sketch two straight lines, on each side of the body, for arms. Sketch ovals for hands.

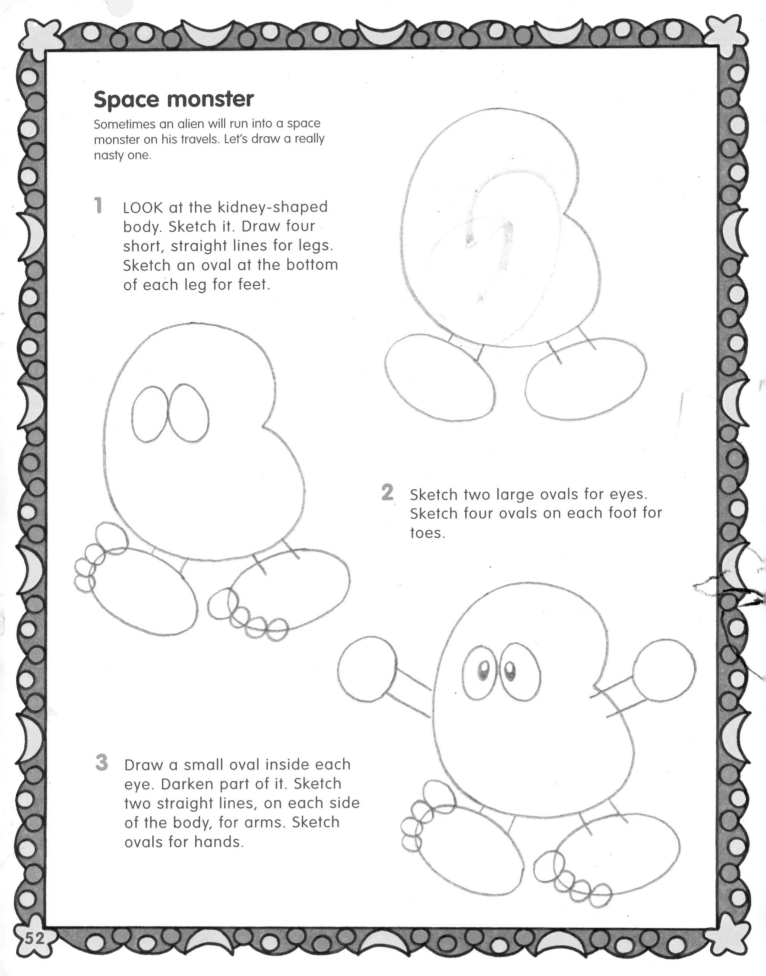

4 Starting at the top, draw the jagged lines for hair. Draw two straight, connecting lines for eyebrows. LOOK carefully at the shape of the mouth. Draw curved lines and straight lines to make the mouth. Draw some circles on his back side. Sketch four ovals on each hand for fingers.

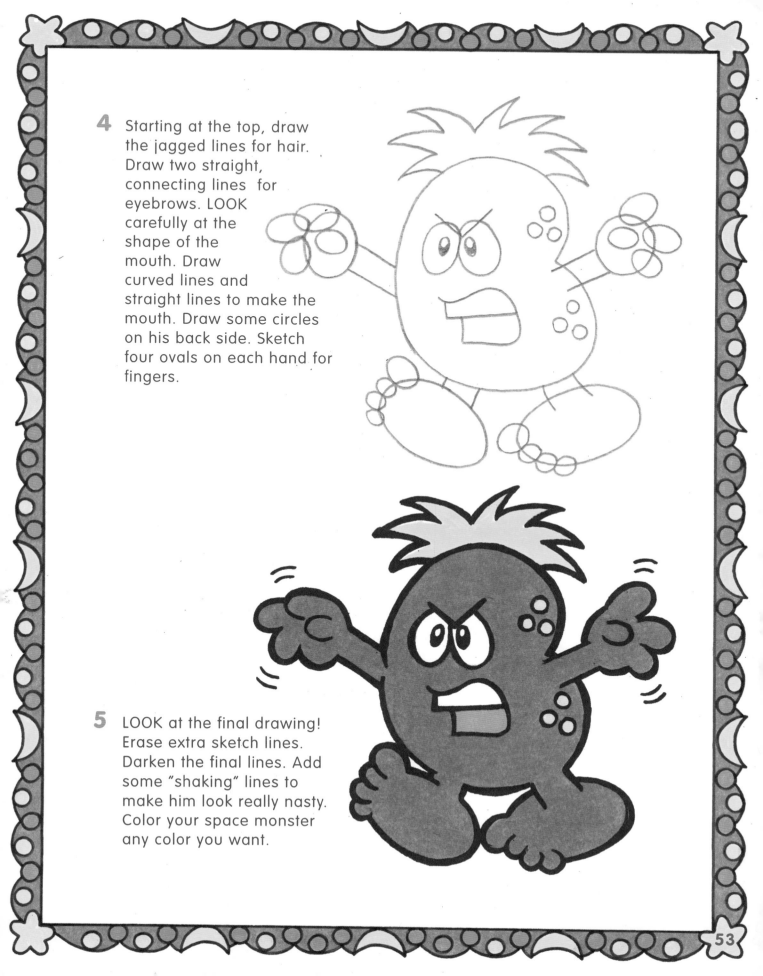

5 LOOK at the final drawing! Erase extra sketch lines. Darken the final lines. Add some "shaking" lines to make him look really nasty. Color your space monster any color you want.

Robot

Spaceships always have robots on them, so let's draw one.

1 Sketch a rectangle, rounded at the top and bottom, for his head. Draw three straight lines for his body. Draw four long straight lines for legs. Sketch two large, overlapping ovals for feet.

2 Sketch a small oval in the center on top of his head. Sketch a small oval on each side of his head. Draw an oval in the middle of his head. Sketch a small rectangle with a circle inside it, in the center of the body.

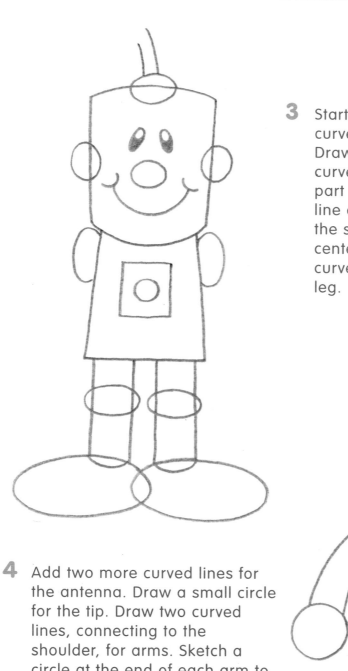

3 Starting at the top, draw two curved lines to begin his antenna. Draw two ovals for eyes. Add three curved lines for a smile. Darken part of the eyes. Draw a curved line on each side of the body for the shoulders. Sketch ovals in the center of each leg. Add a small curved line at the bottom of each leg.

4 Add two more curved lines for the antenna. Draw a small circle for the tip. Draw two curved lines, connecting to the shoulder, for arms. Sketch a circle at the end of each arm to begin the hands. Draw a curved line on the bottom of each foot.

5 Draw small curved lines on each of his arms. Sketch four small ovals on each hand for fingers. Draw curved lines on each of his legs.

6 LOOK at the final drawing! Erase extra sketch lines. Darken the final lines. Color your robot.

GREAT JOB AGAIN!
You just keep getting better and better.

Space worm

Space worms are friendly little creatures that crawl all over space. Many aliens keep them as pets. Let's draw one.

1 Sketch five overlapping ovals for the worm's head and body. Draw two curved lines on top of his head to begin his antenna.

2 Add a small circle for the tip of the antenna. Draw an oval for the eye. Darken part of it. Draw two small curved lines to make his mouth. Draw curved lines and ovals on his back and tail.

3 LOOK at the final drawing! Erase extra sketch lines. Color your space worm.

Sketch, doodle, play!

Experiment with a variety of shapes and lines to create your own cartoon space creatures. Draw squares and triangles and circles and see what you come up with. You can have lots of fun creating strange creatures nobody has ever seen before.

57

Fun stuff to do with your alien characters!

Sketch an alien on a thick sheet of paper. Add color. Draw a rectangle under his feet. Cut around the alien and rectangle. Fold the rectangle back, along the shoe line, under your alien. Stand the alien on a table or desk with a flat surface. You can use him as a room decoration, or make a bunch of them and use them as toys to play games.

Draw an alien on your lunch bag. Sign your name under the drawing so everyone will know you drew it (and they will also know not to eat your lunch!). Take it to school so all your friends and teachers can see how talented you are!

Fold several sheets of paper in half to make a book. Write your own story starring your cartoon alien characters. Write your name on the front cover so everyone will know who wrote it. Share it with your family and friends.

You can also fold a sheet of paper in half and make a decorated greeting card. Draw an alien on the front and write a message on the inside. It could say things like "Hope Your Birthday is Out of this World!" Make up other neat sayings to write in your cards and give them to people who are special to you.

Draw an alien cartoon strip

You can have lots of fun drawing an alien comic strip. Cartoon alien characters talk using something called a word balloon. It is a sort of bubble that appears over the alien's head. It makes it seem like the alien is speaking.

1 Start by drawing two rectangles side by side. You can use a ruler to get the lines straight.

2 Draw two aliens facing each other. Leave enough room inside, at the top of the rectangles, to write their conversation in later.

Try to think of a funny joke that one alien could tell another alien. It can be a funny joke you have heard or one you make up.

3 Draw ovals above the aliens' heads. Add small straight lines on the bottoms of the ovals, pointing the lines toward the alien that is speaking.

4 LOOK at the final drawings! Erase extra sketch lines. Darken the final lines.

5 Write the words each alien is saying in the word balloons.

Great job!

CONGRATULATIONS!
You are officially trained to draw aliens and other space stuff!

Sign and date all of your drawings. Save your drawings in a folder. Later, when you practice, practice, practice... compare your earlier drawings to your new drawings. You will see great improvements! If you do a drawing you are really proud of, sign it and give it to a friend or family member. When you see it displayed, you will know your cartoon made someone else happy.